READING POWER

EVANDER HOLYFIELD
Heavyweight Champion

Rob Kirkpatrick

The Rosen Publishing Group's

New York

1

To the reading teacher.

Published in 2000 by The Rosen Publishing Group, Inc.
29 East 21st Street, New York, NY 10010

First Edition

Book design: Maria Melendez

Photo Credits: pp. 5, 7, 9, 11, 21 © Al Bello/Allsport; p. 13 © Ezra Shaw/Allsport;
p. 15, 17, 19 © Jed Jacobsohn/Allsport; p. 22 © Elsa Hasch/Allsport.

Text Consultant: Linda J. Kirkpatrick, Reading Specialist/Reading Recovery Teacher

Kirkpatrick, Rob.
    Evander Holyfield : heavyweight champion / by Rob Kirkpatrick.
    p. cm. — (Reading Power)
Includes index.
SUMMARY: Introduces the champion boxer, Evander Holyfield.
ISBN 0-8239-5542-7
1. Holyfield, Evander Juvenile literature. 2. Boxers (Sports) — United States Biography
Juvenile literature. [1. Holyfield, Evander. 2. Boxers (Sports) 3. Afro-Americans
Biography.] I. Title. II. Series.
    GV1132.H69 K57 1999
    796.83'092—dc21
    [B]
                                                                    99-16069
                                                                      CIP

Contents

Evander Holyfield is a boxer.

5

Evander boxes in a ring.
Lots of people go to see
him box.

Evander wears a robe
before he boxes.

Boxers fight in rounds. They rest after every round.

10

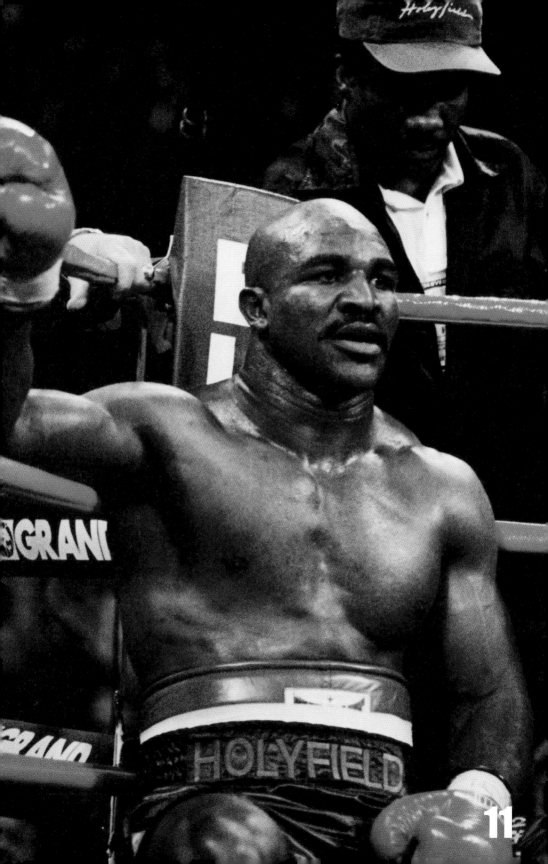

Evander jumps rope.
Jumping rope helps
Evander stay fast.

13

In 1996, Evander boxed Mike Tyson.

Evander beat Mike Tyson in a fight. Evander was very happy.

17

When Evander fights Mike Tyson, he has to move fast. Mike throws big punches. Evander throws big punches, too.

Boxers like Evander and Michael Moorer get close in the ring. They keep their gloves up.

21

Boxers get belts when they win titles. Evander has won lots of belts.

Here's a good book to read about boxing:

Combat Sports (Olympic Sports) by Robert Sandelson Crestwood House (1991)

To learn more about boxing, check out this Web site:

http://www.boxingonline.com

Glossary

belts (BELTS) What boxers get when they win fights.
ring (RING) The place where two boxers fight.
round (ROWND) The time when a boxer boxes in the ring.
title (TY-til) An honor a boxer gets when he is the best.

Index

Word Count: 108

Note to Librarians, Teachers, and Parents

If reading is a challenge, Reading Power is a solution! Reading Power is perfect for readers who want high interest subject matter at an accessible reading level. These fact-filled, photo-illustrated books are designed for readers who want straightforward vocabulary, engaging topics, and a manageable reading experience. With clear picture/text correspondence, leveled Reading Power books put the reader in charge. Now readers have the power to get the information they want and the skills they need in a user-friendly format.